ISBN 978-1-935786-80-1

Printed in the United States of America

St. Clair Publications
P. O. Box 726
Mc Minnville, TN 37111—0726

http://stclairpublications.com

Cover Design

Kent Grey—Hesselbein Design Studio
www.kghdesignstudio.com

DOG TALES OF MARY & MARTHA

By: Mary & Martha (with P.J. Bradley)

StCP

Dedication

We, Mary and Martha dedicate this book to our family: grandparents, Pawpaw and Grandma Lou Lou, our aunts Cheryl, Bob, Judi, Bev and Kiddle, our uncles Gus, Tom and David, and our cousins. Most of all, we dedicate this book to our Mom, who was not afraid to adopt two crazy puppies that would change her life forever. We love you Mom!

M & M

Acknowledgements

Before we were even born, one of Mom's friends lost her husband. Mom said it was just awful. It seemed nothing she could say or do would help. Not long after that, Mom lost her dog Alice. She grieved for Alice for a while, but then adopted us. Lucky for her, we turned out to be two really good dogs.

Mom got the idea of us sending notes of encouragement to her friend. So we, being good obedient dogs, did just that.   To our surprise, we started getting e-mails back from Mom's friend, we now call Aunt Bev. Aunt Bev asked Mom to send her some of our baby pictures.   She thought we were cute and our e-mails and puppy pictures made her smile. After a while, we added more of Mom's friends to our e-mail list. One of the couples we included raises Labs in Tennessee. They sent one of our letters to a publisher who said he might be interested in putting a small book together. That's how all this book writing business got started.

We would like to acknowledge our biological parents and siblings. Abby, our biological mom, was a full blooded Black Lab.   Bubba, our biological dad, was a not so full blooded dog of questionable decent. They fell in love and produced a litter of thirteen beautiful puppies. If it weren't for them, we wouldn't be here.

Most importantly, we acknowledge and thank everybody that has become a part of our lives. From the beautiful hills of Tennessee, to the magnificent Texas Gulf Coast we are truly blessed with family and friends. Thanks to our Aunt Cheryl, a 5th grade teacher who helped proofread our book. Thanks also to Uncle Gus who made this book computer friendly. Finally, a special thanks to Alice, a most excellent dog, who took care of Mom until we could get here.

   Mary   &   Martha
(Great Hunter) (Running Wind)

5/26/2014

Contents

1 About Alice 1

2 The First Letters to Aunt Bev 3

    Hello Again – It's Mary Elizabeth 4

    Aunt Bev's Reply 6

    Little Green Lizards 7

    Dear M & M – Aunt Bev's Reply 9

    New Crates 10

    Thanks from Aunt Bev 11

    Martha's a Blessing 12

    Training & Aunt Cheryl's Blow Up Pool 14

    Aunt Bev's Reply – Still Healing 16

    Shiny Eyes 17

    Birthday Greeting For Aunt Bev 19

    Reply to Birthday Greeting 19

    More Words of Encouragement 20

3 Big Dark Thing with Glowing Greenish Eyes 21

4 Aunt Judi's Reply to Big Dark Thing 23

5 Bath Time 24

6 Martha's Take on Baths 26

7 Yard Bubbles 27

8 Mary's Hurt Leg 28

9 Running Wind Passes Wind 30

10 Turtle.. 32

11 Obedience School... 35

12 High Traffic Areas... 38

13 Double Decker Forward Head Over Heels Roll!!!!............................. 40

14 Ghost Rat 42

15 Squirrel Alert! 44

16 Queen of the Deck 47

17 Bye-Bye 50

18 RABBIT!! 53

19 Squirrel in the House! 56

20 Aunt Cheryl's House 59

21 Runway.. 62

22 Vet Visit... 64

23 Just Looking at the Sky.. 67

24 Just Looking at the Sky -- Again 69

25 MARY AND MARTHA GALLERY 71

1 About Alice

Martha Here!

As most everybody knows, everything about life on Archer Road is gooder than good. Mom takes most excellent care of us; we are happy and feel secure. In the evenings as the sun is setting and things are cooling down, Mom sits out in the yard and talks with us. One evening Mom told us about Alice (Mom's dog before us).

Alice's full name was *Alice Black Dog.* Alice was the name of a lady Mom used to sing with in the church choir. "Black Dog" was the Indian name Mom gave especially to her. How cool is that? I'd rather have an Indian name than a Bible name. I would be called, *"Running Wind"* because I run like the wind. Mary would be called *"Stinking Fish,"* since she likes to swim and all.

Alice could run like the wind too, and was a wader like me. During those days, there were some big catfish in our pond and Alice would creep out in the water and pounce on them. Mom said once she caught one. While she loved to fish, she also kept the yard clear of squirrels and rabbits.

Alice was a street puppy. A nice lady found her wandering around alone and took her in. Me and Mary believe there is a special place in Heaven for people who rescue puppies from the street. Mom needed a dog, and Alice needed a Mom, so it was a perfect fit.

Alice was about 8 years old when she hurt her back. Mom took her to the Vet, but the treatments and medicine were not working for her. For Alice, the nights were long and dark. Mom stayed with her deep into the night. One night while she was laying in Mom's arms, trying to get some rest, Mom whispered a promise in her ear. She promised that she would do everything she could to make things better and when the time came, she would make the right choice to end the pain and suffering. Mom spoke with the Vets one final time, and on September 24, 2010, Alice went to Heaven.

Martha Out!

1/15/2014

2 The First Letters to Aunt Bev

My Name Is Mary

Dearest Aunt Bev,

You haven't met me before. My name is Mary. I have a sister named Martha. We were named after two human sisters that lived back in the olden days, when Jesus walked the earth. It seems he had a friend named Lazarus who had two sisters named Mary and Martha. Since we are sisters and all, we got stuck with those names.

We just got adopted by our Mom and are getting settled in here on Archer Road. We just love it! There are all kinds of things to chase and a pond where we can swim. All is well in our world.

Mom thought it might lift your spirits to hear from us. We don't know much about humans yet, but we are learning more and more each day. We had to say goodbye to our biological Mom recently. We realized as we drove away in Silver Truck that it was the last time we would ever see her. It was sad, but was something that we had to do to move forward. The good news is we have found our new home to be a safe and caring place. Me and Martha believed it then, and believe it now; the best is yet to come.

Oh yeah, Mom is enclosing some of our puppy pictures so you can see how we look.

For Always,

Mary

2/11/2011

Hello Again – It's Mary Elizabeth

Dearest Aunt Bev,

Hello again; it's me, Mary Elizabeth! Yes, my middle name is Elizabeth. I only hear it when I get in trouble. I also hear other words I don't know the meaning of in a not-so-pleasant tone. Elizabeth is also my Cousin Sarah's middle name. Martha's middle name is Louise, also our Grandmother's middle name. Our Pawpaw just calls us M & M when he walks us. He says we are just a couple of little dogs, and don't need those fancy names. I know he's right, but don't tell Martha. I like being a dog, but Martha wants to be a dancer. I keep telling her she has two left feets and it just won't work.

I will ask Mom to send you some updated pictures. I have grown some since my last letter. Yesterday Me and Martha got a bath. Mom tried to get us into the tub by trying to teach us to go up a ramp. We were too smart for that. I knew we might be in trouble when she pushed me out of the bathroom and kept Martha with her. So Martha got her bath first; when she was done, Mom pushed her out and chased me down. It took me a long time to get my "smell" just right. Now I will have to start over.

I told Martha all about you after our bath. She is going to drop you a line soon. Our trainer is coming this Friday to help us learn to walk on the leash better. We really stink at leash walking. Martha told me that if God wanted us to have leashes, we would have been born with one attached to our collar. I'm wondering how come Mom doesn't have one. Bet you never thought of that! Bet Mom hasn't either.

I gotta go now. Need to go for a swim in the pond. Mom will send more pictures and Me and Martha will write and tell you all about the trainer. I wonder if she has a leash?

For Always,

Mary Elizabeth

3/15/2011

Aunt Bev's Reply

Dear M & M,

Thank you for thinking about your poor Aunt Bev. I really appreciate your message. I'm sorry that you got involved with an owner that believes in cleanliness. What a bummer. Make sure that she takes baths in a timely manner also.

I need to know who your trainer is. My little girl, GiGi, is in need of a lot of training. She is almost a lost case. Let me know if you girls like this trainer person. I think that both of your names are just perfect. I do think that "Blue Eyes" should have been included as part of your name. You both do have beautiful blue eyes.

Maybe I'll have the privilege of meeting you both before you go off to college. If not, maybe I'll be invited to your weddings.

Love to both of you!

Aunt Bev

3/16/2011

Little Green Lizards

My Dearest Aunt Bev,

I'm Mary's sister, Martha Louise. Mary told me all about you after our bath the other evening. I wanted to drop you a line to say hello and let you know how we are doing. We are OKAY for now, but as you know, our trainer will be coming to our house this afternoon. Wish us luck. Me and Mary really stink at leash walking. We do pretty good coming when Mom calls, sitting and standing, and basic commands. It's those stupid leashes that don't seem to be working for us. Please pray that the idea of leash walking will come to us soon. It will make our Mom very happy. When she's happy we're all happy.

Last evening Mom was putting our crates back in the house for bedtime. There were two little green lizards snoozing in one of our crates. Mom saw them and says to me, "Martha! Look! Two little green lizards! Go get them, girl!" Mom was all excited. She kept chanting "Get them, girl! Get them!" over and over. I made direct eye contact with her several times. I could tell she wanted me to do something, but what to do? What to do? The more I sat and looked at her, the louder she got.

I was sure I could do "it," if I could just figure out what "it" was she wanted me to do. In my defense, I'm just a puppy. I don't know what "green" means, and I surely don't know what lizard means. So there I was, watching Mom shake the crate all over the place like she was trying to get something to drop out all while chanting, "Get it, girl! Lizard!"

Mary (nowhere to be found) had never mentioned anything about lizards. Junebugs, yes; lizards, never a word. Mom was getting frustrated and tired from shaking that crate for so long, but FINALLY something

7

dropped out. It was small, had eyes that blinked, and most importantly, it would fit in my mouth. So, that's what a green lizard is!

Lizard was dazed, because of all that shaking, and didn't move at first, but when I sniffed it, it moved, and moved very fast, right back into the crate. Mom raised her voice and said in a not-so-pleasant tone, "What self-respecting dog can't catch a little green lizard?!" All new words to me, but I recognized the tone. Thinking on my feets, I decided to run and hide until Mom cooled off.

I think today I will go hunting for some of those green lizards, now that I know what they are. Mary can keep her old junebugs.

It was good to meet you and I will let you know how our training is going. Mary sends her love.

For Always,

Martha Louise

3/18/2011

Dear M & M – Aunt Bev's Reply

Dear M & M,

Please excuse my delay in answering your recent doggie gram. Early Sunday morning my phone rang; it was more bad news. You know I recently lost my husband, now his brother has died. I had to go help his sister make the arrangements for the funeral and stay with her a while. I was extremely sad for days. We have lost three out of that family in less than a year. The only thing that makes me laugh is my GiGi. Tell your Mom to keep praying for me and my family. I do appreciate it.

I'm sure you girls are getting more beautiful each day. Send more pictures. Remember your Mom's bark is worse than her bite (I hope). Hearing from you and looking at your pictures makes me smile.

Love You,

Aunt Bev

3/27/2011

New Crates

Dearest Aunt Bev,

It's me again, Mary Elizabeth. How are you and your wonderful little dog GiGi doing? I am so sorry to hear you are sad again. Please keep on keeping on. You can do it; GiGi needs you! Someday after Me and Martha learn not to jump all over our guests, we can meet and eat some Mexican food. Yes, Me and Martha like Mexican food and ElToro's is just down the street!

Because of this beautiful weather, we mostly get to stay outside. Before my bedtime, I sit up under one of the outside lights and catch junebugs. Martha can keep those lizards; they are just too green for me.

Mom bought us two brand new dog crates. They are extra large and have plenty of room for us to relax. I know they are roomy, because we got baths again this past week and Mom had to go inside of Martha's crate to fetch her. I thought Mom might get stuck, but she managed to retrieve Martha. I'm not sure why Martha gives Mom so much grief about her bath.

Mom told us we needed to sleep in our own crates. I think that's a good idea since Martha is in trouble most of the time. I went to get my beauty rest a couple of days ago, and Martha climbed in my crate with me to snooze. My head was all cramped up, and I couldn't stretch out, but Martha is my sister so I didn't say anything. Mom looked in on us later and didn't like the way I was all cramped up so she "encouraged" Martha to move into her own crate. Much to my surprise she moved, so I got to stretch out all over the place. Mom watches how we nap and sleep closely. She told us Alice (Mom's dog before us) hurt her back and she doesn't want that to happen to us. That means a lot to Me and Martha.

As soon as we figure out what "a back" is, I'm sure we will appreciate it even more. We are learning new words every day.

You take care of yourself. I will tell Mom to give you another call. She knows how hard it must be for you this time of year. Stay out of trouble and take good care of GiGi for us. Martha sends her love and will write soon.

For Always,

Mary Elizabeth   3/28/2011

Thanks from Aunt Bev

M & M,

Thank you for the flowers! I'm wondering if Martha has a broken paw since I have not heard from her lately. Keep the letters coming, girls! You must be getting bigger and bigger each day.

Love you,

Aunt Bev

4/1/2011

Martha's a Blessing

Dearest Aunt Bev,

Martha Here!

Thank you for thinking about me. My paws are fine. In fact I dug up one of Mary's bones and munched out on it, so my paws are in good shape. I'm so glad you liked the flowers! It was all my idea. Mom and Mary have no taste at all, so I had to pick them out and everything. I'm glad they made you smile.

Smile is a new word for me. Mom said it is what humans do when they are blessed. Blessings can come from anywhere, and make lots of people smile. Mom said I was a "Blessing." I make her smile. Now that I think on it, being a "Blessing" is better than being a dog. "Blessings" put Mom in a good mood. Someday I hope Mary can turn into a "Blessing" too.

Our trainer called Mom again, so we will be in training this Friday. We have been leash training and trying to fetch things. Mom tried to leash walk us at the same time. It wasn't pretty. I went one way and Mary went the other, and Mom went down. We were all tangled up in our leashes and Mom was saying some words we didn't know in a not-so-pleasant tone. She managed to unhook us from the leashes and laid there on the ground with us a while. The next time I saw a leash, it was on my collar, and Mary wasn't wearing one. Mom takes us leash walking one at a time now. We are getting better and better at it each day. I'm sure I will get even better now that I'm a "Blessing."

Mom and Aunt Cheryl (her sister) are going to see our Aunt Bob (another sister) in some place called Fort Worth. Alice's Aunt Judi is going to stay with us. Mom doesn't leave us by ourselves overnight, and Aunt

Cheryl didn't want to ride 5 hours in a car with us. It will be OKAY; we love our Aunt Judi too. She brings us treats and sits out in the yard with us and watches us play. She thinks we are great! I can't wait till she sees what a "Blessing" I've turned into.

I gotta go. Mary just ran by with something in her mouth. She's pretty fast. So if I wanna see what she has, I've got to catch up to her and pounce on her. No rest for the weary. Take care of yourself and take it easy.

For Always,

Martha Louise

4/6/2011

Training & Aunt Cheryl's Blow Up Pool

Dearest Aunt Bev,

Martha Louise Here!   Happy Mother's Day!

Man, are we glad it's May! Me and Mary had a lot going on in April. We got fixed and had to take it easy for a while. Mary got an infection a few days after surgery, so she had to go back to the doctor. She's better now. Grandma Lou Lou and Pawpaw stayed with us a few days — spent the night and everything. They seemed to know a bunch more about little dogs than Mom does, for sure. Grandma took care of Mary when Mom was at work, and at night too. Pawpaw let me sleep on the couch with him, after Mom went off to bed. We only got busted once. It was great!

We both are growing pretty fast. Mary weighs a few pounds more than I do; she's at 42 pounds now. Our trainer has been coming to the house and helping Mom understand more about how young dogs think. She likes us a lot and kisses us on the head. We are working on our basic commands and have one more lesson this week. We are supposed to be mastering the fetch command. We just don't get it. Mom says FETCH! Then she throws one of our toys out in the yard. We run after it and go bury it. Me and Mary heard the trainer talking about it. We are thinking we are supposed to be bringing our stuff back to Mom when she throws it out like that. I still don't get it. If she wants to keep the stuff, why does she throw it out in the yard in the first place?

Aunt Cheryl gave us a small blow-up swimming pool. It seems that Alice (Mom's dog before us) used one for years to take her bath in. She never bit it or popped it, just stood in it while she got her bath. That was Alice.

Mom blew up our three-ring pool yesterday and tried to teach us how to get in it. It was sad. She really tried, but we just didn't get it. Finally she chased Mary down and threw her in. Mary loved it. I took a closer look at the pool and the cool water, and decided I wanted a piece of that pie. It was great! Me and Mary played for hours. In and out, out and in, biting, snipping, jumping, barking, standing on the sides of the blow-up rings with our sharp toenails. Long story short, we now have a one-ring pool. I'm guessing we will have a hard plastic one by nightfall.

Let us hear from you.

For Always,

Martha Louise

5/9/2011

Aunt Bev's Reply – Still Healing

Beautiful Ladies,

Please excuse me for being so neglectful. I enrolled in a "Future Teachers of Adults" class recently, so for 7 weeks I've been tied up with the study. I spent 8-10 hours studying all of the literature that I could. I purchased a computer package and read and studied that. I got the Music Department to get me the words to a song "He Has Been Faithful to Me." I cried just a bit, but was able to read (not sing, my little ones) the words to the song to my class. I had most of the class crying and then they applauded me at the end. On Monday I was so tired and empty that I hardly moved.

I don't open my computer every day, so it might be a while before I read your letters. I'm still trying to find my way, but am so much better. It is encouraging to see your letters when I open up my computer. Keep them coming.

Hope your Mom had a good Mother's Day. Being the mother of twins is a difficult task. Did you both act like nice, sweet ladies? That is the way I like to think about you. But I think your Mom is special, so what do I know?

Good bye for now; keep the letters coming.

Love you,

Aunt Bev

5/25/2011

Shiny Eyes

Dearest Aunt Bev,

Martha Louise Here!

It was good to hear from you! Congratulations on the new class. Good for you. Your church is most fortunate to have you there.

Me and Mary hope you had a good Memorial Day. We sure did. Mom put a flag up and everything. She was off from work four straight days. It was great!

We finally had our last lesson with our trainer for a while. We learned how not to mall Mom's guests when they arrive. We learned how to sit and wait until it was time for us to "formally" meet somebody. Mom was impressed. We were doing pretty good until Aunt Kiddle came over to see us. We just couldn't stand it and forgot everything we knew and jumped and barked all over the place. Aunt Kiddle just laughed. Mom was really embarrassed, so we practiced sitting and waiting for an hour after Aunt Kiddle left. We are also practicing something Mom calls "GO!" We like it because that means Mom is coming with us while we run in the BIG YARD. We love it when Mom comes with us, because we can show off our stuff. Mom says we run like the "wind." We are not sure what "wind" is, but we run like it, so it must be good.

Every morning around 4:30 Mom takes us out to look for RABBIT!! She has a spotlight she uses to scan the yard for shiny eyes. When she catches the shiny eyes in her light, she yells RABBIT!! When that happens, Me and Mary are supposed to run like crazy towards the shiny eyes. I saw RABBIT!! once, but was too slow to catch him. It's really fun for me and Mary to chase after RABBIT!! Right now we really stink

17

at it, but we are getting faster and faster each day. Someday we will run faster than RABBIT!!

Mary sends her love. Right now she's in the doghouse. Mom caught her snoozing on the couch again. I told her she would get caught, but she just won't listen.

Write when you can and let us know how GiGi is doing.

For always,

Martha Louise

5/31/2011

Birthday Greeting For Aunt Bev

Dearest Aunt Bev,

Happy Birthday! Our birthday wish for you: May you catch a thousand RABBITS!! May you always have God's blessings upon you! May you never have fleas. May you run like the wind in a large fenced-in yard. May all be well in your world for always.

M & M

6/1/2011

Reply to Birthday Greeting

Dear M & M,

Thank you for remembering me on my 76th birthday. Already my age or something is catching up with me. I've had TMJ problems and went to the dentist for some relief. I'm going to my primary doctor for some more help in the morning. Did your trainer teach you how to pray? Please learn as quickly as possible; I need it. Sorry, need to close for now.

Love you both,

Aunt Bev

6/14/2011

More Words of Encouragement

Dearest Aunt Bev,

Mary Here!

We learned to pray early on. Mostly because we got in trouble a lot and needed God's help every hour. God has been good to us both and just keeps blessing us all over the place. We will pray that you get better and better and maybe God will send you a RABBIT!!

Sorry to hear about your TMJ problem. We hear it is painful. Mom had a problem with a root canal and her jaw was hurting pretty bad, but it is better now. She gets all cranky when she doesn't feel well. We will pray for you both.

Keep in touch and let us know how you are feeling. Before long, you will be running in the yard and eating everything in sight.

For Always,

Mary Elizabeth

6/14/2011

3 Big Dark Thing with Glowing Greenish Eyes

Mary Here!

Martha isn't feeling well. It's not her fault. Mom said so. I think she's going to be alright, but for a while last night, we got really scared. To understand why Martha is not feeling well, we need to go back a few months, just after we came to live on Archer Road.

It was a happy time for all of us, Me, Mom, and Martha. Mom kept us in a pen in the kitchen during the day so we would be safe. Our grandparents came over to check on us and exercise us while Mom was at work. All was well in our world.

In the evenings, Mom had us sleep in the living room on our pillows while she snoozed on the couch. Her friends in Tennessee that raise Labs told her how to house train us. She followed their advice and always went out with us so we would be safe.

Martha began the practice of standing on her hind legs with her front paws on the couch to gently wake Mom when we needed to go outside. Mom never got mad at Martha for waking her; in fact she praised us both for being so considerate.

When we were about 6 months old, we moved into what Mom called a "bedroom" to snooze. She bought us new pillows and put them at the foot of her bed, so now we have several places in the house we can snooze without getting in trouble. Still, to this very day, Martha wakes Mom in the same way, standing on her hind legs with her paws next to Mom to gently wake her. That is, until last night.

So there we all were—Me, Mom, and Martha—the first evening in our bedroom, snoozing like crazy. On Mom's night stand there was an alarm clock with a lighted dial, a flashlight, her cell phone and a glass of water. Martha woke up and needed to go outside for a few minutes, but here's the deal: Martha is much bigger now, so when she stands on her hind legs; she stands over Mom and looks down on her. Martha has a beautiful dark brown coat, with eyes that now, because of the light from the alarm clock, have an eerie greenish glow. Before I could stop her, Martha woke up Mom.

Mom, who had been in a deep sleep, didn't see Martha when she opened her eyes. She saw **A BIG DARK THING WITH GLOWING GREENISH EYES LOOKING DOWN AT HER.** Not pretty! Now I've heard Mom's not-so-pleasant tone, I've heard her laugh, but I've never heard her scream like that. Man, was she upset! Mom threw her glass of water on Martha and tackled her. Martha was startled and tried to get out of the way. We were all bumping into each other trying to get out of the room, when Mom realized it was just us and started calming down.

Martha was so upset she forgot what she woke Mom up for. I just ran and hid in my crate. When all was quiet, I came out and ventured into the living room where I found Mom sitting on the couch, and Martha sitting in front of the couch (at a safe distance). They sat there for a while, just looking at each other.

As they sat there in silence, Martha remembered what she woke Mom up for and went over to the door where we both went out to take care of business. When we came back in, we got to eat some yogurt and some snacks. Mom kept saying we were good dogs and how she appreciated Martha waking her like that. Maybe so, but we're thinking we will most likely will be waiting until morning now to take care of our business.

Mary Out!

8/2/2011

4 Aunt Judi's Reply to Big Dark Thing

Aunt Judi Here!

Mary! What an exciting experience you and Martha and Mom had. I was wondering if you are still going out in the middle of the night these nights. Sounds like your Mom was sleeping really hard, so I guess it is not good to wake her "suddenly" when she is in a comatose state. Maybe you and Martha could get some dark glasses for such an occasion, that way your Mom wouldn't see those green eyes staring at her. I know you both are good girls, and I hope to see you sometime soon. I like the way you are both protecting Mom and loving her. Please don't get too hot outside in this weather.

Love you,

Aunt Judi Out!

8/4/2011

5 Bath Time

Mary Here!

It was a great weekend for Me and Martha. January 7th is a day of celebration! One year ago on this date, we came to live here on Archer Road. I remember it well; we ran like banshees all over the place. We didn't get in trouble all day long. It was great! Mom told us we made her very HAPPY! We don't know what Happy! is, exactly, but Martha thinks it's like how you feel when you get jerky treats and run like crazy all day in the BIG YARD. All day Saturday we celebrated and had a fine time.

We snoozed well into the morning. Sunday was a most beautiful day. Our Aunt Judi came over to help Mom bathe us. The day was warm, and breezy, but Mom was concerned that we might catch cold, so she made us a bath in the hall bathroom. Martha was placed in our pen so Mom wouldn't need to chase her down when it came time for her bath. Mom doesn't have to chase me down, because I'm much better at taking baths and swimming than Martha, so I always go first. Mom just calls my name, no leash or anything. I'm good like that.

Mom and Aunt Judi lifted me up and put me in the human tub. It was warm and relaxing. Mom bought us some new shampoo that wouldn't hurt our eyes, would sooth our skin, and smelled like apples. Now I don't know what apples are, but Mom seemed to like the smell, so it was okay with me. So there I was, all lathered up, smelling like apples. I didn't give Mom or Aunt Judi any grief. I took my bath, got rinsed off, got some treats and got all dried off. I was feeling good! Now it was Martha's turn.

Martha has never been good at taking baths. I ran out to the pen to tell her not to worry, but IT WAS TOO LATE! Martha was a wreck. I kept talking to her, but the more I talked, the more upset she got. Mom put Martha on her leash and had to drag her inside to the human tub. She didn't know what apples were either, but she didn't want to smell like them. She gave Mom and Aunt Judi all kinds of grief. I had to stay outside the bathroom in the hall, but I was hearing all kinds of noises thru the door.

I heard several swats, and a raised voice in a not-so-pleasant tone. Martha would not stand still in the tub. There was a bunch of racket. I heard Martha whining and splashing. I heard that not-so-pleasant tone, all the while smelling those stupid apples. Then there was silence. It was so quiet I thought Martha had gone to Heaven.

Finally the door opened and a ruffled Martha pranced out. Mom and Aunt Judi were soaked. Martha took off running, giving them more grief, so they chased her down to dry her off. After all that was done, we went for a walk to finish drying off. Me, Mom, Martha, and Aunt Judi, all walking in the BIG YARD, smelling like those stupid apples.

Mary Out!

1/9/2012

6 Martha's Take on Baths

Martha Here!

I am writing to set the record straight. Mary is giving me grief about our bath time. For starters, it wasn't as bad as Mary said it was. Me, Mom, and Aunt Judi had a little misunderstanding. That's all it was. For the record, I don't mind baths. Deep in my heart I know they are good for me and they do make me stop itching and feel better. Baths are not a problem as long as I don't have to get wet and all lathered up. Mom and Aunt Judi just misunderstand this concept. They need to figure out a way to give baths without soap and water. How hard can that be?

Martha Out!

1/10/2012

7 Yard Bubbles

Mary Here!

So there we were snoozing in our beds, smelling like those stupid apples when blue lights started flashing all around. Martha woke up first. BOOM! BOOM! Time to wake up, Mom! BOOM! BOOM! FLASH! FLASH! FLASH! Mom came in the room and told us we were okay. FLASH! FLASH! FLASH! BOOM! BOOM! We may be many things, but okay wasn't one of them. Mom told us it was just a thunder storm. We really didn't care what humans called it, we didn't like it. It was too loud, too flashy, and hurt our ears. Mom moved our pillows over by the couch and stayed with us until we got back to sleep.

The next morning, we found our yard full of water. Martha put her nose in the water and blew some bubbles. How cool is that? Yard bubbles! So we blew bunches and bunches of yard bubbles all over the place.

Hold it! What's this? A little animal just floated up. Mom was most impressed; she called the little animal a crawfish. So there Martha stood, nose to nose with one of those little things. She must have spooked it because it snapped at her and caught her nose with its pincher. Martha was shaking her head like crazy. Finally the little crawfish flew off Martha's nose and the race was on! We chased those little crawfish all over the place. When we lost one, we blew more yard bubbles to flush out another. When Mom left for work, we didn't even notice. Me and Martha will be busy blowing yard bubbles and chasing crawfish all day. How cool is that?

Mary Out!

1/12/2012

8 Mary's Hurt Leg

Martha Here!

Today Mom went out to run some errands. I'm not sure what an errand is, but when Mom comes back from running them she gives us treats. We are glad she runs errands, but do not understand why she uses Silver Truck. When we run, we use our feets.

While Mom was away, Mary hurt her leg. It wasn't my fault this time. When I chew on Mary, I chew on her back legs; they are much easier to get to. I get in trouble for doing it, but I forget sometimes in the heat of battle. I'm just a dog, and it's not like Mary doesn't chew on me.

By the time Mom got home, Mary was limping pretty bad. Mom picked up on it fast, and wouldn't let Mary come outside with me. Mary got to lie in the BIG CHAIR with her feets up for the REST OF THE DAY! Mom tried to figure out where Mary was hurt, so she gave her a look-over. She looked and looked and looked all over Mary's paws and leg, mashed around on her, and talked very calmly and gently to her. Mary just sat there all calm and gentle too, being all nice and sweet. MADE ME SICK!

Mom had some pain medication for Mary she got from the Vet when Mary hurt her leg the last time, so she gave Mary a dose of it. We both got a treat. Mary got one because she had to take her medicine. I got one because I'm just a good dog. Mom thanked me for not jumping all over Mary while she was hurt. I just figured it would take both of us to help get Mary well.

For the rest of the day, Mom walked Mary slowly with her harness and leash. She didn't let her run like a banshee even when I found that cat next door. I felt bad for her, but Mom let her stand with me by the fence and bark like crazy. Later on, Mary just wanted to lie down in the sun.

Mom thought that was a good idea because it would give us a chance to practice camping. So there we were, lying there practicing camping. Mom was rubbing our ears and telling us how good we were. How cool is that? I think we are going to like camping.

This morning Mary is much better. She is moving slow, but not limping. Mom fed us our favorite food and went to work. I'm going to be careful with Mary today so she will get better and better so I can start chewing on her again.

Martha Out!

1/23/2012

9 Running Wind Passes Wind

Mary Here!

So Mom and Aunt Kiddle went to a place called Canton, Texas. We heard them talking and Mom said it was the home of the largest flea market in the world. Me and Martha aren't too sure why humans would want to buy and sell fleas at some market, but we have found humans do many things we don't understand.

Mom asked Aunt Judi to dog sit with us while she and Aunt Kiddle shopped for fleas. So she did. We had a great time! Aunt Judi brought us some cool treats and a couple of **BIG BONES** to chew on. She also let Martha sleep with her in the human bed. They snoozed and snoozed each night until it was time for our morning run. I must admit, Martha looked and felt better when she snoozed with Aunt Judi. Next time, I might just climb in the human bed with them.

When Mom got back we were very happy, so was Aunt Judi. In fact, when Mom drove in and parked Silver Truck, Aunt Judi started up her car and drove right out the gate. She told Mom that we were good dogs and she knew we needed some alone family time to get re-acquainted. Aunt Judi is thoughtful in that way. Then poof! Aunt Judi was gone.

We never saw any fleas, but we told Mom all about how much fun we had with Aunt Judi. Mom walked with us out in the **BIG YARD** for a long time. She watched me swim, and we ran like banshees all over the place. As the sun went down, we went in to watch Rin-Tin-Tin on TV and eat some supper. When it was time for bed, Mom brought out some brand new **BIG** sleep pillows she had picked up at the flea market, nearly too big for our crates. To be safe, Martha checked them for fleas before she settled down to snooze. So there we were again. Me, in the living room, Martha in her crate in Mom's room, and Mom in the human bed next to Martha. All was well in our world once again.

We all fell into a deep sleep. Snoozing, snoozing, snoozing, UNTIL Martha *passed some wind.* I was awakened by some movement in Mom's room. It wasn't Martha, she was fast asleep, it was Mom, choking, coughing, and calling Martha's name. Martha snoozed on. I keep telling her not to eat a big supper and go to sleep. She does it all the time. Usually, we are outside and it's no big deal, but this time it wasn't outside.

In just a few seconds, I began to smell the problem. It came down the hall like a rushing river. On first sniff, I knew I wanted outside and fast. Then I heard more noises from Mom's room.

Mom said in a loud not-so-pleasant tone "MARTHA! MARTHA! MARTHA! GET UP, GIRL, TIME TO GO OUT!!!"

As I waited by the door, I heard a loud, shaking sound, like Mom was trying to dump Martha out of her crate. Still, Martha snoozed on. I thought the paint might start peeling off the wall and was concerned for Mom. My eyes were watering and I had shortness of breath, I can only imagine what she must be going through. Still Martha snoozed on.

Finally, I heard one final MARTHA! in a crazy, loud, not-so-pleasant tone, and here came Mom and Martha running down the hall. Mom threw open the door and we all ran outside into the fresh air! We walked around for some time in the cool night air before going back inside. Back inside, we all settled down to sleep, and all was well in our world once again.

Mary Out! 2/15/2012

10 Turtle

Martha Here!

I must say I am impressed with Mary. She does swims like a fish. I need to learn to swim, but I'm afraid to jump off in the water like Mary does. She's fearless. Even when I try to push her back in the water as she's trying to get out, she manages to push me up and over. She's very strong. This weekend when I tried to pounce on Mary as she was getting out of the pond, she ducked and I flew right into the pond. It was spooky. I saw my life flash before my eyes and everything. I think I might have seen Jesus. Most likely, Mary did it on purpose; she really wants me to learn how to swim.

This weekend, while we were out in the **BIG YARD**, having our family time, Mary found something that was moving along the back fence line. She called me over to take a look. We didn't know what it was, but we knew what it wasn't. It wasn't a cat, rabbit, coon or skunk. It had no hair or feathers. It was hissing and snapping at us as we sniffed and pawed it. It was trying to get out of the **BIG YARD**, so I decided to call Mom so it wouldn't get away. Mom was managing a fire ant mound, and didn't come right away when I called her, so I sent Mary over to get her. I saw Mom squatting by a very large ant mound spreading something over it. She was concentrating so hard she didn't see or hear Mary. Mary, thinking quickly on her feets, went right over to Mom and barked really loud right in her ear. Not a good choice.

As Mom was hastily brushing off the ants, I kept calling for her to   look at this thing Mary had found. She finally looked up and started making her way to the fence. I was right on target, pointing like crazy, balanced on three feets. Mary came up and joined me, standing on her three feets and pointing like crazy. Mom came up, smiled, and PICKED THE THING UP!

Mom said, "Ladies, this is very good. You have found a turtle!"

WOW! WE FOUND A TURTLE! WOW! CAN WE KEEP HIM?! CAN WE KEEP HIM?!

Our turtle was hissing and snapping while Mom held him. She walked over to the pond, let us sniff him one more time, and then dropped him in the water and BAM! HE WAS GONE! Mary jumped in after him and looked all around while I searched the shoreline. We kept looking for him as Mom went back to the ant mounds.

A few days later, we found Turtle trying to escape again. We pointed like crazy till Mom came out. This time she picked him up and brought him to Blue Pool where he couldn't escape. After she took a picture of him, she picked Turtle up and put him in the pond again. BAM! Just like before, he was gone under the waves. I hope he doesn't get out while Mom is at work, he might just escape. Oh well, such is life. I need to move on to other things. Me and Mary are having a meeting this afternoon on how to keep the lizard and frog population under control in our yard. It's a thankless job but someone has to do it.

Martha Out!

3/19/2012

Mary & Martha check Turtle out in Blue Pool

11 Obedience School

Mary Here!

A few weeks back I heard Mom on the phone talking to our trainer. When we were puppies, this trainer lady came over to Archer Road for about 7 straight weeks and tried to convince us that walking on a leash, sitting and staying were good things. I remember it was a big deal because our grandparents and Aunt Judi came over to watch us train. I didn't see any of them on leashes or sitting on the cold ground. We did sit and stay for them just to please them, but we still stink when it comes to leash walking.

Anyway, a few weeks back, the trainer lady called Mom and asked her if she wanted to sign us up for obedience school. Mom said, "Sure, Mary and Martha would love to go to school." Now Me and Martha don't know what school is, but if that trainer lady is there, it can't be good. We learned early on, that what we think doesn't matter, so like it or not, Mom signed us up for 7 more straight weeks of that stupid leash stuff.

The time for our first class came around. We knew something was up, because Mom was all nice to us. She came home, put our harnesses on, crates in the truck, packed us a bag and gave the UP! command. Being good dogs, we got in our crates when she told us to, and we all drove out to the Rodeo Fairgrounds, where aunts Cheryl and Judi were waiting.

Aunt Cheryl has a crazy street dog named *Jack* that eats other animals. Mom's not too fond of him. *Jack* showed up for school, and was getting signed in when we got there. Mom got me out of the crate, put my leash on, and handed me off to Aunt Judi who was going to be my trainer for the evening. *Jack* saw us and the other dogs unloading so he started barking like crazy and tried to get away from Aunt Cheryl. Mom was about to get Martha out of her crate when JACK BROKE FREE. Not only did he break free, he came over to Silver Truck all growling and barking and STARTED CHEWING ON ME! Mom was yelling, Aunt Judi was yelling, Aunt Cheryl was yelling and Martha was barking like crazy. Mom quickly gave the UP! command for me to get back in the truck and to the safety of my crate. I tried to follow that command, but JACK CHOMPED DOWN ON MY LEG, DRUG ME OFF THE RAMP, AND STARTED CHEWING ON ME! SOMEBODY DO SOMETHING!

Mom was beyond upset, and was on her way down to knock Jack into the middle of next week, when the trainer's husband pulled Jack the Animal Eater off me.

Mom gave me a "look-over" to see if I was hurt. When she didn't see any blood, she started calming down. Aunt Cheryl came over and gave me a "look-over" too. She felt bad about what happened and was going to leave and take Jack home, but Mom asked her to stay.   If anybody needed obedience training it was Jack.

Me and Martha finally got down on the ground. THEN we had to put on our "gentle leaders," another type of leash that fits over our head, which is very uncomfortable. THEN a bunch of other dogs started showing up. Everybody was sniffing everybody and barking like crazy. THEN there was Jack the Animal Eater at a safe distance pulling Aunt Cheryl all over the place. It was sad. I just wanted to go home, but nooooooo, we stayed on.

The real nightmare began, when the trainer started barking orders out. Aunt Judi and Mom walked us around in circles, all everywhere, up down, all around. Mom ran backwards and Martha followed, Aunt Judi

36

ran, I ran, Martha sat, I sat, Aunt Judi sat, then everybody got up and ran forward, even *Jack the Animal Eater* ran, we halted, then did it all over again. About halfway through the class, Mom swapped Martha for Me. It seemed like hours had passed when I looked up and saw our grandparents in the crowd watching us. It was good to see them. They clapped for us and told us we were good girls. Pawpaw helped Aunt Cheryl with *Jack*, which was good because *Jack* and Pawpaw like each other. It's a guy thing. *Jack* seemed calmer when Pawpaw was with him, which was good for Aunt Cheryl.

Finally, Me and Martha both came to a place where we said enough is enough. I had done all I could do. It was hot, bugs were everywhere. I was finished for the evening. Mom knelt down beside me and told me I did just fine and gently rubbed my head. Martha saw us from across the arena, and came over to where we were dragging Aunt Judi behind her. As the trainer was finishing up, Mom whispered to Me and Martha that she was proud of us and thanked us for being good dogs. Were we relieved! She sat there with us on the floor of that arena as we leaned on her for support.

After a quiet walk in the BIG YARD we went inside to our pillows and crashed. Neither one of us moved until the next morning. I don't know how long seven weeks is, but it's too long for me.

Mary Out!

10/5/2012

12 High Traffic Areas

Martha Here!

It wasn't entirely our fault. Who would have thought it? Why did Mom get upset with us Sunday afternoon? To explain, I need to go back when we were younger and didn't know any better.

When we were puppies, Mom house trained us. It took us a few months, but we learned to go outside to take care of business. This pleased Mom greatly. It pleased her so much that we decided to follow the example that Alice (Mom's dog before us) set. It seems that Alice avoided what Mom refers to as "high traffic areas" in the yard. Mary told me if we sniffed around we could find out where Alice took care of business. So we sniffed around and found that Alice always went to the back part of the yard along the fence line. I must say, this was very impressive. The problem we had was most of the day we are in our smaller yard and don't have access to the BIG YARD. Our yard is nice too, so if we need to go before Mom gets home, we just go over to the side of our yard, a non-high traffic area, and take care of business. It's been working fine for us until this Sunday.

When we were just puppies, squirrels would taunt us. Now that we are all grown up, no squirrel passes through our yard, which means they no longer hang out in Mom's old pecan tree either. This year, that old tree produced what Mom called a bumper crop. Mom makes pecan pies for our boy Jacob, so she was very pleased to see all those pecans. She even thanked us for taking care of the squirrels.

So there was Mom, picking up pecans, thousands of them all over the ground. Mom got a rake and was raking them all in. She was so excited, I was excited, and Mary was excited! We all love pecans! All was well in our world.

The thing is, in our world, we never considered underneath the old pecan tree to be a "high traffic area." When Mom raked up all those pecans, that's not all she raked up. Me and Mary were lucky she was wearing gloves. We got a lecture about how we needed to put that location on our list of "high traffic areas." Mom's okay, because she's getting thousands of pecans, and it's because we chased off the squirrels, so we are forgiven. The important thing is all is well in our world once again.

Martha Out!

10/8/2012

13 Double Decker Forward Head Over Heels Roll!!!!

Martha Here!

Good morning to all! It's a most beautiful day. Me and Mary are all frisky. The moon was nearly full last night and we could see everything as we romped through the grass in the **BIG YARD.** It is a most excellent time of the year! It is also a time when we tend to get in trouble a lot. It's not our fault, we are just dogs. We are always learning about humans and their way of life. A good example of that happened to us this very cold morning.

So last evening, we snuggled up on our big pillows. We got all warm and peaceful and fell into a deep sleep, snoozing for hours. All was well in our world. Then that beeper thing Mom calls her alarm clock went off, and we all got up. Me and Mary were all rested up and ready for the day. Mom let us out and we just couldn't believe how **BEAUTIFUL** the moon-lit morning was. We took care of business and then chased each other like crazy dogs around our front yard. We do something we call a DOUBLE DECKER FORWARD HEAD OVER HEELS ROLL!!!! That's when, as we are running like crazy dogs, we meet up, crash into each other, hold on and roll through the grass till we stop. Together we weigh over 140 pounds, so when we roll, we roll hard and fast. We were practicing our DOUBLE DECKER FORWARD HEAD OVER HEELS ROLL!!!! when Mom came out for our morning walk. We could tell she too was enjoying the cool weather and beautiful moon. She gave the "GO!" command, so Me and Mary did just that. Mom had the spotlight, so there we were, walking in the moon light with Mom looking for shiny eyes. All was well in our world.

Me and Mary decided to warm up and trot around a little. Our trots turned into a run, and then we decided to DO IT! OUR DOUBLE DECKER FORWARD HEAD OVER HEELS ROLL!!!! It was just perfect! We jumped and met up in mid air, just like we practiced, and hit the ground rolling.....rolling....rolling very fast...and then THUMP! We hit something! UH OH! The loud hard thump was MOM! Mary! We took out Mom! Oh No! We both got up and went to see if we had killed Mom. Who was going to feed us? Take us to the Vet?

It didn't take us long to figure out Mom wasn't dead, we were in trouble, and we were standing too close to her. She was really ticked and came up out of the grass yelling some colorful words in a not-so-pleasant tone. One word started with an "S". As we were running for our lives, Mary asked me what the "S" word meant. I told her, "How should I know what STUPID means? Just run!" Mom didn't say much as she left to go to work. We could tell she was moving a little slower than usual. We will be more careful next time we do our DOUBLE DECKER FORWARD HEAD OVER HEELS ROLL!!!! Like I said, we are just dogs. Me and Mary are really hoping that all is well in our world when Mom comes home. You guys might want to keep us in your prayers. Thanks!

Martha Out!

10/29/2012

14 Ghost Rat

Martha Here!

This morning, as usual, Mom let us out for our morning run. When we were done, we went back and waited for Mom to come walk with us. All was well in our world, or so we thought.

Mary saw *IT* first, just on the other side of the human gate on our driveway. *IT* was round and white. She started barking all over the place and yelling for me to come. I could tell by her bark, she was spooked, so I ran (like the wind) over to see what was up. The closer I got, the more spooked I got.

I didn't know what to do, so I started barking all over the place too. I told Mary to keep *IT* on the other side of the fence while I went and got Mom. So while Mary continued to bark and jump all over the place, I banged on the door with my paw. No Mom. I barked loudly. No Mom. I banged on the door and barked loudly. No Mom. Then Mary, who had been barking all over the place, **STOPPED BARKING!**

OH NO, *IT* GOT MARY!! I KNEW IT!!! *IT* MUST BE ONE OF THOSE GHOST RATS! MARY WAS SO YOUNG! BEAUTIFUL MARY! GONE! EATEN BY A GHOST RAT!!!! MOM! MOM! MOM! MOM! WHERE ARE YOU?? A GHOST RAT HAS EATEN MARY! *IT* WILL EAT ME TOO! THEN *IT* WILL EAT YOU! AND WHO KNOWS WHO ELSE *IT* WILL EAT! GHOST RATS ARE LIKE THOSE ZOMBIES UNCLE GUS TOLD US ABOUT! THEY EAT DOGS!

I was exhausted from all the yelling, when Mom finally came out and in a quiet orderly fashion started making her way over to the human gate. Sometimes Mom is just too human for her own good! Can't she see this is an emergency!?

"WHAT DO YOU THINK I'VE BEEN OUT HERE BARKING ABOUT?" I yelled. "You took your sweet time! Now the GHOST RAT has eaten Mary!"

Then Mom, like she was fearless or something, started going right up to the human gate. I tried to stop her, barking and jumping around like crazy. DON'T DO IT, MOM! DON'T DO IT! Mom raised her voice, and in a not-so-pleasant tone, told me to "HUSH!" She boldly walked over to the place where I last saw my Beautiful Mary. I followed at a safe distance and then heard her ask, "Mary, what's was going on, girl?"

MARY! IT CAN'T BE, THE GHOST RAT ATE HER! I came out from behind Mom, and there was MARY! *AMAZING!*

Mary started barking and pointing like crazy. Wait a minute! She was taking all the credit for finding the GHOST RAT and showing it to Mom. Mom was making over Mary like she had done something special. Good Girl; Good Job; Good Grief! MADE ME SICK! Stupid Mary.

Then Mom took the chain off the gate and went out and PICKED UP THE GHOST RAT! *AMAZING!* As she was coming back in the human gate Mary jumped and grabbed it, and took off. I ran after her in case she needed help chewing on it.

When I caught up to her, my heart was beating fast, I was hoping I had enough strength left to chew on the GHOST RAT.....hey wait a minute......this isn't a GHOST RAT! This looks like a white sack with a big yellow "M" on it. I've seen this before when we munch out on Chicken Nuggets! Stupid Mary.

Martha Out!

11/8/2012

15 Squirrel Alert!

Mary Here!

It was a Sunday. Things were quiet, too quiet. We had just eaten lunch and settled down with Mom for our Sunday afternoon snooze. We were nice and cool and could see the front yard from our beds. All was well in our world.

So there we lay, looking out the window. Waiting and watching for that stupid SQUIRREL. We don't like SQUIRREL. He looks like those big gray field rats that come up in our yard to steal our food and water. SQUIRREL is just a BIG RAT with a fluffy tail. For the record, I don't have a problem with snakes, lizards or junebugs, but I have no use for squirrels or rats.

Anyway, there we lay. Martha heard it first. She jumped up from a deep snooze, pounced on top of me where I lay by the window, and started scanning the front yard. Mom was still snoozing on the couch; she heard nothing.

"Did you hear that?" Martha whispered.

"Hear what?" I answered. But just as the words came out of my mouth, I heard something, by the big willow tree, a few yards out, and it sounded like SQUIRREL!!!!

"Let's make sure before we wake up Mom," Martha suggested.

Then BAM, we saw that FLUFFY TAIL; first to the left, then to the right, then to the left, then to the right. "MARTHA, I THINK WE CAN CATCH HIM! WE NEED TO GO NOW!!!!! WAKE UP MOM!!!!" I whispered.

Martha was wayyyyyy ahead of me. She alerted Mom with the *"SQUIRREL ALERT." MAYDAY! MAYDAY! MAYDAY!!!! OPEN THE DOOR, WE GOTTA GO! SQUIRREL ALERT!!!!*

Mom didn't look too happy, as she sprang up from her deep snooze. Her hair was all stacked to one side of her head and her eyes were puffy. She didn't have her glasses on, so I was really hoping she wouldn't trip over Martha who was dancing around sounding the *"SQUIRREL ALERT!"* Sure enough, on her way to open the door she TRIPPED OVER MARTHA, but managed to catch herself. When she regained her balance, Martha had doubled back and was jumping all over the place barking the *"SQUIRREL ALERT!"* over and over and over. Unfortunately, Mom lost her balance again and fell back over Martha, luckily on the sofa.

I'M NOT BELIEVING IT; MOM......QUIT MESSING AROUND AND GET THE DOOR OPEN!!!!

Mom was saying some words we've never heard before, in a not-so-pleasant tone, and now she was limping. Finally the door opened and we flew out barking and running like crazy.

Running like the wind, Martha went to the left, and Me to the right of the big willow tree. Then Martha bumped into SQUIRREL...FACE TO FACE! SQUIRREL did an about face and instead of going up the tree like he usually did, he ran to the right of the willow tree and face to face with ME! I TOOK MY PAW AND SLAPPED HIM DOWN....HE ROLLED...he must have been dazed, because he ran back toward the base of the willow tree.......not very bright! MARTHA WAS WAITING AND TOOK HER PAW AND SLAPPED HIM DOWN! He was really dazed but managed to get up again, and still he did not go up the tree like he usually did, he took off across the yard toward the fence where we both knew the fence would

45

stop him.....so we (both running like the wind) went after him.....Martha went to the left, and I to the right and chased him around in the weeds by the fence, slapping him down, biting at that fluffy tail.....then he took off again back towards the willow tree with us in hot pursuit........then HE FELL AND LANDED ON HIS BACK SCREAMING AND BITING AT US AND WE AT HIM.......he was nearly ours, when he managed to make a weak leap to the base of the tree and got up just out of our reach.......wounded, heart beating rapidly, just out of reach, but he knows now, we mean business, we aren't puppies any more.

Our hearts were pounding; we nearly had him. We will have him next time, mark my words. We stayed at the base of the willow tree for hours just in case he fell or decided to come back down. Mom came out and took a look up in that tree. (She wasn't limping as bad now, but her hair was still all stacked to one side.)

Mom said, "My, my, girls, you did good. You worked as a team, and nearly had him. Come inside, cool off and chew on a fresh piece of rawhide."

WE LOVE FRESH RAWHIDE! Man! Mom must be real impressed!

Martha even said, "Mary, you did good!" That was really something coming from her. From that day forward she never called me "Stinking Fish" ever again. She now calls me "Great Hunter."

Mary Out!

11/12/2012

16 Queen of the Deck

Martha Here!

Greetings to all! Me and Mary hope all is well in your world, it is in ours. At least now it is. Mom is doing much better this morning, and that is good news for us all!   That ibuprofen stuff works wonders. I'm glad she took a bunch of those softgel things last night; she needed to get some sleep after it happened. We are relieved she is **OKAY.**

You may be asking, what happened? It happened last evening, just as the sun was going down. It had been a most beautiful day. The sunset was beautiful too. Mom was running a little late getting home, and Me and Mary were getting a little worried.   Then we heard Silver Truck! **SHE'S BACK!**   Man we miss her when she leaves! We are always **EXCITED** to see her! Sometimes maybe a little too **EXCITED.**

Mom opened the door and we swarmed in like two crazy banshees. Barking and jumping all over the place. She wanted us to calm down and eat our supper. **NOT THIS EVENING! WE WERE WAY TOO EXCITED!** So Mom said, "Okay girls, let's go walk first."

This was a good idea for everybody. Me and Mary aren't sure why, but sometimes we get so **EXCITED** we can't seem to get a hold of ourselves and forget how to follow commands. Don't know why that happens to us, but Mom knows just what to do. She either takes us for a walk, or if it's really bad, we get a lecture in a not-so-pleasant tone.

Mom opened the back human gate and out we went. We ran all over the place, chasing birds, sniffing for **RABBIT!!** We ran and ran and ran some more. We even did a couple of our *DOUBLE DECKER FORWARD HEAD OVER HEELS ROLLS!!!!* They came out just perfect. All that running had calmed us down and Mom asked us to come in and eat some supper. It

47

sounded reasonable to us, so we trotted up to the house. That's when Mary challenged me to a Queen of the Deck duel. And why not? We had some time; Mom was behind us at a safe distance.

BAM! Mary knocked me off the deck! I got up and chased her down. BAM! I hit Mary; she rolled! I POUNCED on her! Missed! Mary circled around behind me! Oh No! She's too fast! Too fast! So I made a quick left roll, then right, then left! BAM! Mary did a body slam and I was down again! The "Circle Chase" was on! Round and round we went! Then right when I was making my body slam, THUD! What's up with this? Mary was still on her feets, so I must have hit something else.

"What did I hit? What's that sound? Moaning? How eerie! By the way, is that Mom on the ground over there, on her back rolling back and forth holding her knee?" I asked.

Mary replied, "Who else would it be Ms. Running Wind, she's the only human here?"

We stopped the Queen of the Deck duel and headed over to where Mom lay.

"Hey, Mom is still making that eerie sound. Why is she holding her knee and rolling back and forth from side to side? I asked."

Mary replied, "You didn't body slam me, you managed to body slam Mom. Smart move!"

WHAT HAVE I DONE!? We went over to Mom to see if we could help her. Mom's face was red, and she was still lying on her back making that eerie sound. She was in a sad state.

"Quick, Mary," I yelled, LET'S SNIFF HER ALL OVER THE PLACE THEN LICK HER ALL OVER HER FACE! THAT WILL HELP HER UP! So we did just that, both of us, at the same time.   It wasn't too long before she was up off the ground. Works every time! Mom was quiet for most of the evening. We gave her the night off and just laid beside her snoozing and keeping her and her knee warm. Thanks to those ibuprofen softgel things, all is well in our world again.

Martha Out!

2/14/2013

17 Bye-Bye

Mary Here!

She really tries. Mom feeds us, plays with us, walks us, takes us to the doctor, gives us our heartworm pills, and even took us to school. She really means well, but I gotta tell you, she really stinks at dog training.

Mom came in from work yesterday and we went out in the BIG YARD to chase some squirrels. When we were done there, Mom let us watch Rin-Tin-Tin as we ate our supper. We just love to watch that handsome German Shepherd in action. He's an officer in the US Army and knows his stuff, unlike that little human Army guy. Rinny really needs to transfer out of that unit and away from that kid. He's always getting Rinny in trouble.

After Rin-Tin-Tin was over, Mom put our harnesses and leashes on and we all went out into the BIG YARD. We walked over to Blue Truck where Mom informed us that she was going to teach us how to go "Bye-Bye."

I glanced over at Martha as she glanced over at me, then we both looked at Mom. What did "Bye-Bye" mean? This was a new word. Was it an animal like RABBIT!!!? A stuffed toy? A place? Where is "Bye-Bye" and why would two good dogs want to go there? So we both did what we always do when we can't run and hide, we looked to Mom for further direction.

Mom knew we didn't get it. So she explained that she wanted us to enter into Blue Truck and sit on the seat in a safe and timely manner. Normally we ride in our crates in the back of Silver Truck, so this was unusual. Mom figured we needed to learn to ride in the cab of a truck in case of an emergency.

So, Martha went in the house, and Me and Mom went over to Blue Truck to train. I learned how to enter Blue Truck and sit on the seat in a safe and timely manner. Then it was Martha's turn, (it usually takes longer with her, that's why I got trained first). Martha learned to enter Blue Truck and sit on the seat in a safe and timely manner too. Mom was very pleased, and told us so.

We practiced it over and over, entering into Blue Truck and sitting on the seat in a safe and timely manner. Then Mom added herself to the mix. Me, Mom, and Martha, all got in and out of Blue Truck in a safe and timely manner, over and over, and over.

Finally we were ready for our final exam. Mom closed the doors to Blue Truck, we went over by the house where she took off our leashes waited a few minutes and then she gave the "Bye-Bye" command. Blue Truck's door opened, Me, Mom and Martha entered Blue Truck and sat on the seat in a safe and timely manner.

This pleased Mom, and she was happy, we were happy, and *THEN.........SHE TURNED A KEY, AND IT GOT ALL CREEPY; A MAN WAS YELLING OUT FROM UNDER THE DASHBOARD THEN THERE WAS MUSIC. WE GOT SPOOKED!!!!! WE BARKED....WE CRIED....WE SCREAMED....WE GOTTA GET OUT OF HERE; WE'RE GOING TO DIE!!! MARTHA JUMPED OVER MOM (WHERE SHE FOUND AN UNOPENED WINDOW AND SMASHED INTO IT) NOT TO BE DETERRED, MARTHA JUMPED BACK OVER MOM, THEN OVER ME (WHERE SHE FOUND ANOTHER UNOPENED WINDOW) THEN I LOST IT TOO!! WE'RE GOING TO DIE!!! MAYDAY! MAYDAY! SPACE TOO SMALL! SPACE TOOOOOO SMALL!!!! WANT OUT! NEED OUT! WILL BREAK SOMETHING SOON TO GET OUT! MOM, DO SOMETHING!!!*

51

When Mom could not calm us down, she said in a very loud not-so-pleasant tone, "It's only the engine and radio!" *WE DIDN'T CARE WHAT IT WAS! WE WANTED OUT!*

Mom did the only thing she could do; she opened the driver side door. Martha didn't wait till Mom exited the vehicle in a safe and timely manner; she pounced over Mom and into the yard where she hit the ground running. I was a little more tactful and waited until Mom exited the vehicle before I made my un-safe and un-timely exit into the yard!

Mom was not pleased at all. When we all calmed down and were watching TV later, Mom told us we were not done with our "Bye-Bye" training yet. Pray for us.

Mary Out!

4/24/2013

18 RABBIT!!

Martha Here!

Mary has not been feeling well and is on antibiotics to clear up a skin infection. The antibiotics are working, and she is getting better and better each day. I don't like it when she's sick. I've never told her, but I think she's the best sister dog ever.

I hate to admit it, but there are several things she is better at than I am. One is swimming, the other is tracking. Mary is persistent and keeps tracking until she finds whatever it is she is tracking, or Mom calls us in to eat. If she finds it, she goes after it with a vengeance. This day was one of those days.

It was a good day. The early morning fog had burned off and the sun was bright and warm. The baby goats that lived next door were up and about jumping around like crazy. We had just finished munching out on our morning treats, and were laying out on the deck soaking up the warm sun. All was well in our world.

Mary said that she thought a Ghost Rat may have taken up residence up under Grandma Lou Lou's old Playhouse. We had been digging for days sniffing things out. To me, it smelled like **RABBIT!!** but what do I know? When we were done sunning, we decided to go find that Ghost Rat.

We began to sniff around and dig out a little more dirt. BAM! Something shot out from under the Playhouse! Something BIG!

WHAT WAS THAT?

"Martha, you were right! It's the **BIGGEST RABBIT!! IN THE WORLD!** *AMAZING!"* Mary exclaimed.

AND THE RACE WAS ON!

Up the fence line! Down the fence line! Mary cut him off so he couldn't get back under the Playhouse. She was great! Around the pecan tree, out to the front fence, along the deck in and out he went. I had no idea RABBITS!! could run so fast, and this was one BIG RABBIT!! Finally, Mary was on one side, I was on the other. Then RABBIT!! tried to throw his body up against the back gate in hopes the gate would open. WRONG CHOICE! RABBIT!! went down! He was ours! He squirmed and squirmed, but Mary held on tight.

By the time Mom got home, RABBIT!! was deceased. Maybe so, but Mary was still carrying him around like a trophy. We did play with him for a long time. If the truth be known, that's probably why he was deceased.

Mom knew something was up, because we weren't at the front gate to greet her. When she came out on the deck, there was Mary standing proudly with RABBIT!! in her mouth.

Mom said, "What a BIG RABBIT!! you guys. Where did you get that? I'm impressed!" That's what she said, I promise.

When Mom called us in the house to eat supper, she went out and buried the biggest RABBIT!! in the entire world. While we were munching out, we got to watch Wheel of Fortune. Man, we had a good day! Got some sun! Got RABBIT!! Got some supper! Is God good, or what? All is well in our world.

Martha Out!

5/1/2013

Mary standing proudly with RABBIT!!

19 Squirrel in the House!

Mary Here!

Please keep us in your prayers; we are both in bad trouble. We didn't know at the time it would cause such a ruckus. It was an honest mistake. My goodness, we are just dogs!

It was about 2:30 A.M. this morning. Martha needed to go outside, so she went to get Mom up. Mom says if she has to get up, we all have to get up. So being the obedient dog I am, I got up and went outside too. There we were, Me and Martha, out in the moonlight, taking care of business; all was well in our world.

About 5 minutes had passed, when all of a sudden, the lights in the house went on. We heard Mom yelling in a not-so-pleasant tone, and then the door flew open.

I looked at Martha and thought, this can't be good. It wasn't. Mom came flying out the door (really ticked), went over, picked up a shovel and went back in the house. This looked very strange to us. Mom uses the shovel when she plants her seeds, and buries stuff we "team catch."

"UH OH!" Martha yelled, "Mary, where did you leave that deceased squirrel?"

"You had it last," I answered, "Where did you leave it?"

There was silence, and I knew right away where she had left it. Earlier this evening, when we came in for the night, Martha brought the squirrel we had "team caught" a few days ago into the house. We always carry our toys around, so when we came in for bed, Mom didn't notice. Martha snoozed with it in her chair all evening. When she got up for her nightly break, she left it there, on the chair, in the house, with Mom.

Mom, who Martha had just woken up from a deep sleep; Mom, who can be grumpy on a good day; Mom, who just came out and got a shovel, now had to do something with a deceased squirrel at 2:30 in the morning. Not pretty.

We had to think fast on our feets, so when Mom was putting her gloves on, Martha MOVED THE SQUIRREL! Not a wise choice. This upset Mom even more; now she had to re-find it, while talking to us about our future in a not-so-pleasant tone. We thought we might be going to Heaven. There was nowhere to hide, so we did the next best thing. We got all still and sat in a quiet orderly manner by the couch where Mom could see we were trying to be real obedient. We dare not move. By that time, Mom had re-found our squirrel, scooped it up with the shovel, and went out the back door, leaving us inside, sitting by the couch in a quiet orderly manner, still being real obedient.

When Mom came back in, she didn't say much of anything. She cut off the lights and told us to go to bed, which we did, in a quiet orderly manner, still being real obedient. I'm guessing we won't be getting any breakfast in the morning. Martha thinks we might become available for adoption soon.

Mary Out!

6/28/2013

"Re-found" Deceased Squirrel

20 Aunt Cheryl's House

Martha Here!

Yesterday was one good day! The rain stopped, and it was ,ooler than usual. Our morning walk went well, and Mom was in a good mood when she left for work. Me and Mary were hanging out in our yard barking at the goats next door, chasing squirrels and pouncing on lizards. All was well in our world.

The day just kept getting better. Mom came home from work in a good mood; we all had some supper, and then rested up under the Great Fan in the living room. After we rested up a while, Mom got up and put our harnesses on us. This could only mean one of two things. One, we were going to the Vet, or two, we were going on a road trip. Mom had already loaded our crates in Silver Truck, so now we were ready to load up and head out.   Mom gave the "UP!" command; we jumped in the truck and got in our crates and took off!

Sometimes we go to the beach, but this day we went over to Aunt Cheryl's house just down the road. Aunt Cheryl and Uncle Tom were out of town, and Mom was watching their house and feeding their 100 year old cats. Since *Jack the Animal Eater* (Aunt Cheryl's street dog) passed away, it's safe for us to go over to Aunt Cheryl's house.

One time when we were there, we found Julie, (one of the 100 year old cats) in the bushes. Uncle Tom scooped her up and took her in the house before we could say hello. Aunt Cheryl's little girl used to dress Julie up in doll clothes and push her around in a stroller. (Me and Mary think that is sad, even for a cat.) With all of Aunt Cheryl's kids gone now, Julie is semi-retired. She's still the House Master, and keeps the other two cats, mice, small snakes and lizards in line, but is taking it easier these days.   This evening, while we were visiting, the House Master was in her house snoozing.

With *Jack* gone and all the cats in the house, we had free rein of the yard. Like I said, the day kept getting better and better. We jumped down from the truck and were off.   Running like crazy dogs all over everywhere and back again. We ran through Aunt Cheryl's pond and up the other side then rolled in the dry grass. Mary found a turtle leg and took off with it, but wasn't quick enough. Mom caught her and made her drop it.   We were having such a good day; Mary didn't give her any grief and just dropped it in the grass and took off for another swim in the pond. This was a good move on Mary's part, Mom had not used her not-so-pleasant tone all day, and this was no time to press our luck.

Running, jumping, pouncing, and wrestling all over the place while barking like crazy. On and on we went for what seemed like hours.

HOLD IT!   WHERE'S MOM?! SHE WASN'T WATCHING US RUN, JUMP, POUNCE, AND WRESTLE! HEY, THAT'S HER JOB, TO WATCH US AND KEEP US FROM EATING TURTLE LEGS!!

So we stopped running, jumping, pouncing and wrestling and went to look for Mom. I ran (like the wind) to the back of the lot. No Mom. I ran (like the wind) to the east, then to the west.   No Mom.   Mary (who doesn't run like the wind) checked the front yard. She picked up Mom's scent and started to track her.

"Come on, Martha, this way!" Mary barked. So we went sniffing all the places Mom had walked. Finally we sniffed our way to the garage and to Aunt Cheryl's back door. She must be in Aunt Cheryl's house!

What could she possibly be doing in there? I didn't know and didn't care but, SHE NEEDS TO BE WATCHING US RUN, JUMP, POUNCE AND

WRESTLE! WE MIGHT FIND ANOTHER TURTLE LEG AND EAT IT AND DIE OR SOMETHING!

So we started barking like crazy dogs, all the while scratching at Aunt Cheryl's back door. WHAT IF JULIE'S EATEN HER!? WHAT IF SHE'S DEAD!? MOM! MOM! MOM! MOM! WE'RE HERE AND NEED YOU WITH US!!!!!

Finally after forever had gone by, Mom came to the back door and told us to "HUSH!" HUSH!? US HUSH!? WE'VE BEEN LOOKING FOR YOU FOR HOURS!!!! DON'T THINK SO!!!!!

Not hushing turned out to be a poor choice. When Mom says Hush! she means Hush! Mom walked us back to the truck, clapped her hands and gave the "UP!" command in a not-so-pleasant tone. Me and Mary spent the rest of the time at Aunt Cheryl's in our crates sitting in a quiet orderly manner. When Mom finally drove us all home, it was in a quiet orderly manner too. By the time we got home, Mom had cooled off, and everything was good. We went inside and watched Wheel of Fortune, all sitting under the Great Fan in the living room. All was well in our world once again.

Martha Out!

7/24/2013

61

21 Runway

Martha Here!

Man! God has been good to Me and Mary! Mary is well and feeling good. Mom is well. We are all enjoying the beautiful weather. Mom has been coming home each evening and working in the BIG YARD. I'm not sure what a garden is, but Mom has one. We don't call that spot a garden, we call it a runway.

Before we were even born, Mom had a new driveway put in to park her trucks on. She had a big load of leftover dirt dumped in the BIG YARD where it sat for a long time. When Me and Mary came to live on Archer Road, we used to run up on top of it and roll down on the other side. Sometimes we'd play "Queen of the Runway!" Those were the days.

A few weeks ago Mom got on our runway with a shovel and started moving some dirt around. Then she put some plants and something she called seeds in our dirt. Me and Mary watched the whole time thinking our runway won't be as tall, but that's okay, it's wider now, it will be easier to run, jump, and pounce off of as we fly thru the air.

I don't understand what planting is, but Mary thinks it's like burying a bone. Hide it, so you can come back later for a snack. It made a little better sense, but then Mom put something she called tomato cages up and partially blocked our entrance ramp. After she was done, and moved on to other things, Me and Mary went to check it out. I told Mary we were going to have to move those stupid cages out of the way. Mary thought that might not be a good idea, so we left them alone...for now. Honestly, I was worried that our runway days were over.

Not to be defeated, I decided to make a run just to see if I could get enough momentum to make the great leap and fly once again. It was a perfect plan. Back up to the fence line, run like crazy, pounce on the mound of dirt behind the tomato cages, make a hard right, and fly into the back yard. What could go wrong?

So I backed up to the fence line, ran like crazy, and pounced on the dirt behind the tomato cages with all four feets. I would of made the hard right like I had planned, except the dirt I pounced on was really soft, so all four of my feets sunk, and sunk **DEEP**. It startled me at first, but I thought, I'll just pull myself out and try again. It was then I found myself stuck. I pulled and pulled on my feets. With each pull I noticed more of the soft dirt was coming out. I began to see some of that stuff Mom had buried to snack on later all over the top of the ground. I had just broken free when I heard Mom yelling at me in a not-so-pleasant tone. I did what I always do when there is danger lurking about. **I RAN FOR MY LIFE!** Man! Mom was ticked! When Mary finally caught up with me, she just shook her head and quoted the unwritten rule of the **BIG YARD**, "Only he who buries the food gets to dig it up."   Wish she had told me that sooner.

Martha Out!

7/30/2013

22 Vet Visit

Martha Here!

It was a hot but most beautiful August day. All was well in our world. Me and Mary were out in our yard all day, watching the goats, pouncing on lizards and waiting for Mom to come home. This day when Mom came in, she put our harnesses on us and got our leashes.

This meant Road Trip! But where? The beach? Aunt Cheryl's? Vet? Mary was thinking it might be to see our doctor. Most unfortunately, Mary was right.

Now I don't have anything against Dr. Scott or Dr. Wendy. I'm just not too fond of the Vet's office in general. The ceilings are high, so when I talk to Mom, it echoes big time all over the place. Mom sometimes uses her not-so-pleasant tone when she tells us to "HUSH." It usually takes a while for us to get into our doctor room, but not this time. Mary had been talking to Mom at the same time I was, and it was getting pretty loud in the waiting room. This visit, we were ushered into our doctor room very quickly.

It wasn't too long before two ladies came in and got Mary. I don't like that, but it happens every time we go. Mom never seems too concerned, but I was. I didn't hear Mary screaming or anything, and they do always bring her back, but I still don't like it. I quit talking; I thought maybe if I stopped, they may forget I was there, which turned out to be an incorrect assumption on my part.

When Mary came back, those same two ladies took my leash, and "encouraged" me to follow them in a quiet orderly manner. Never a good thing. Mary told me they checked her poop and did her nails. Oh man! I HATE the poop test.

64

While I was gone, they put Mary on the table for her look-over. Mom was concerned about a little hole in Mary's heel, and a patch of "something" that had come up on one of her feets. Mary had a strange skin infection a few months earlier that had just healed, and Mom thought it might be coming back. Anyway, while I was out taking my poop test and getting my nails done, Dr. Wendy came in to give Mary her look-over. I figured by the time I got back, Dr. Wendy would be ready for me, my second incorrect assumption for the day.

Dr. Wendy kept looking at Mary's legs and feets, then she looked in her ears, then she gave her shots, then she looked back at everything again. All the while she was looking at Mary, she was telling her what a beautiful dog she was, how clean her teeth were, how pretty her coat was, on and on. MADE ME SICK! Come on now! Get her done!

I was ready for my afternoon snooze, so I laid down right there in the doctor room and started my nap. Just as soon as I dozed off, I heard Dr. Wendy call my name.

"Come on Martha," Dr. Wendy said, "it's your turn, girl."

It's about time! Mary's not the only dog that's got stuff going on. Since Dr. Wendy liked Mary so much, I was planning on giving her some grief, but when she told me how beautiful I was, I decided against it. I let her look at my feets and teeth, and way down into my ears. I didn't move one muscle, not one muscle! Dr. Wendy told Mom my left ear was all red and I needed some drops. HEY! I need some drops! How cool is that? Mary usually gets all the medicine.

Mom stood by me while Dr. Wendy gave me my look-over. Mom even bragged on me. She told Dr. Wendy that I didn't eat carbohydrates, that's why I maintained the perfect weight for a dog my size.

"What do you mean Martha doesn't eat carbohydrates?" Dr. Wendy asked.

Mom said, "I mean she won't eat bread or chips, things like that, and Mary does."

Dr. Wendy asks, "And why does Mary? Chips don't fall off the shelf into her mouth do they? Who gives Mary chips and bread?"

Busted!

Mom got BUSTED by Dr. Wendy! Wow! I didn't see that coming! Mom admitted that she and Mary would sometimes snack in the evenings while watching TV. I'm thinking SOMETIMES?

Mom and Mary munch out on all kinds of things while we are watching T.V. I don't like the taste of those things, so I don't eat them. Then Mom got the unabridged version of Dr. Wendy's food lecture and how it wasn't good for her or Mary to eat such things. I was most impressed with Dr. Wendy. Especially since I wasn't in trouble.

Finally my look-over was done. Me and Mary both got some medicine this time. I hope it tastes good and will make me run faster.

Martha Out!

8/2/2013

23 Just Looking at the Sky

Martha Here!

I don't know how it is in the rest of the world, but in our world August is really hot. Even at night, it's hot. Our Mom realizes how hot we can get, so she brings us in the Big House while she runs errands and we snooze under the Great Fan in the living room. We always have fresh water, and sometimes she puts something called ICE in the water that makes it really cold. It helps us stay cool and focused.

One August evening Mom put a chair and some other stuff in the back of Silver Truck. This was unusual for a work night. Highly unusual, because it was such a hot August night. She got in Silver Truck and drove it to the middle of the BIG YARD where we chase rabbits and squirrels. After she parked Silver Truck, she let down the tailgate and climbed up in the bed of the truck and sat down in the chair and just started looking at the sky. She was there for a while, by herself, sitting in that chair in the back of Silver Truck just looking at the sky.

Me and Mary didn't know what to think. So we just watched her for a while, as she sat in that chair in the back of Silver Truck just looking at the sky.

Then Mom called us. So we trotted over to the truck and stood on our hind legs to see what she wanted. Mom had our travel mats all laid out in the bed of Silver Truck. She had some treats for us and a cold bottle of ice tea for herself. She gave the "up" command, so we jumped up in the bed of the truck, and laid on our mats.

So there we were, Me, Mom and Mary, sitting out in the back of Silver Truck on a hot August night, in the middle of the BIG YARD with Mom just looking at the sky. As we sat in the darkness, I looked over at Mary, and she looked at me, and then we both looked at Mom, who was still just looking at the sky not saying anything. We thought she might be watching for Jesus, but there would be a bunch more light and angels and stuff all around. Anyway, it's a tad early for Him yet.

We were growing more and more concerned, so I decided to do something. I put my front paws up on Mom's knees and stood up on my hind legs and looked her right in the eyes and barked at her.

Mom looked right back at me and said, "No worries, guys, tonight there is a meteor shower and I am hoping to see some falling stars."

OHHHHHHH! That explains everything, Oh! Falling stars!

Just what is a falling star? Why would it be falling out of the sky? As we sat there for a while longer, I'm thinking she must looking for Jesus and we need to stay close. I don't want to get left behind.

So Me and Mary sat close to Mom, Mary on her right, and Me on her left. Mom put her hand on our heads and rubbed our ears, as we sat in the back of Silver Truck, on a hot August night, just watching for Jesus.

Martha Out!

8/12/2013

24 Just Looking at the Sky -- Again

Mary Here!

We just love Christmas time! There is excitement in the air. The family comes over during the season and Mom prepares a feast. Everybody tries to make it home for Christmas, and this Christmas everyone made it home for at least a few days. We ate like high-dollar dogs, and then we snoozed. It was great.

After Christmas was done, the family all went home, and Mom went back to the daily grind of getting up and going to work. Today, Mom came home early from work and spent a lot of time out in the **BIG YARD** with us. Then we all went in for supper and to watch Wheel of Fortune. So there we all were; I was snuggled up with Mom on the couch, and Martha was on the big pillow beside us. Then Mom **FELL ASLEEP.** This was unusual because it was still daylight outside. Rarely does Mom fall asleep during daylight, and rarely by me. So I did everything I could to make her comfortable. I rolled over to her as close as I could, and put my head on her head to keep her from getting cold.

So there we were, snoozing like crazy. After a long while, Mom woke up and seemed surprised that she had been asleep so long. She jumped up as she looked at the human clock and said, "Good, we haven't missed it."

"Missed what?" I thought.

She put a lawn chair and our big pillows out on the driveway. Then she got our chair blankets and put them out on our pillows. All of this was highly unusual. Me and Martha went outside for our late evening run. When we got back to the driveway, there Mom sat, with her bottle of ice tea **JUST LOOKING AT THE SKY.**

69

Looks like we are going to be watching for Jesus again! Mom called Me and Martha over and gave the "sit" command. Which, being well disciplined dogs, we did. This wasn't so bad. We could keep an eye on the yard (and the sky) sitting on our pillows which kept our feets warm. We got all comfortable and Mom put our chair blankets over us and we were nice and toasty.

So there we were in our yard with Mom, all nice and toasty, watching for Jesus, when all of a sudden there was a bunch of pops, booms, and all kinds of noise all everywhere. Flash! Flash! Flash! The sky was all lit up all over the place. All kinds of colors! *AMAZING!*

This must be the big day! Jesus must be on his way in! The sky is all lit up; there must be angels around someplace. Could it be?   Mom got up from her chair and started walking all around the yard JUST LOOKING AT THE SKY.   Not to be left behind, Me and Martha jumped up and started running around and barking like crazy!   Boom! Boom! Boom! Flash! Flash! Flash! It was just *AMAZING!*

We all went and sat down, waiting for the Lord to show up. The flashes and booms started to taper off. Mom was smiling as she looked down and said, "Happy New Year Girls!"

All is well in our world.

Mary Out!

1/2/2014

Mary and Martha, 6 Weeks

Mary at 3 Months

Martha at 3 Months

Mary and Martha with Babies

Martha and Mary, 6 Months

Mary and Martha by Pond

Great Hunter and Running Wind, 7 Months

Running Wind (Martha), 1 Year

Great Hunter (Mary), 1 Year

Mary under Chair Blanket, 2 Years

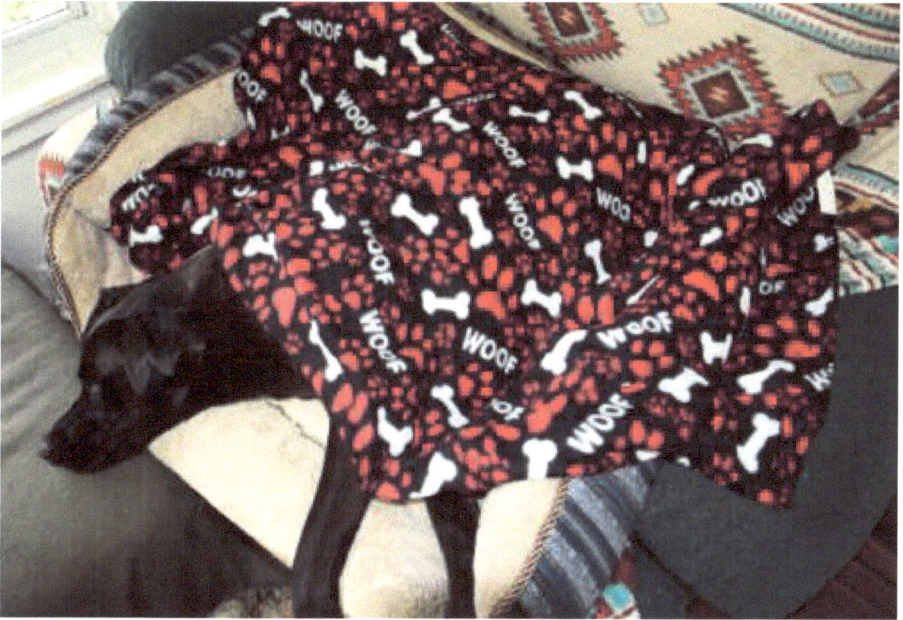

Martha Snoozing under Chair Blanket, 2 Years

Girls Helping Pawpaw, Uncle Gus & Uncle Tom with their Fence

Martha Taking Off with Fence Supplies

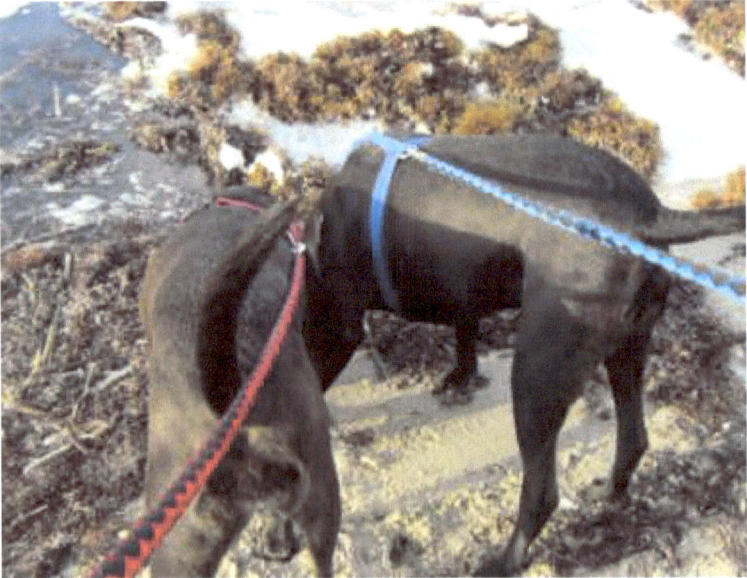

Beach Dogs

Close Up of Turtle

Great Hunter - Running Wind with First Snake

www.ingramcontent.com/pod-product-compliance
Lightning Source LLC
Chambersburg PA
CBHW051238090426
42742CB00001B/12